SHIPS

Alan McGowan

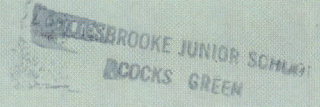

Macdonald Educational

How to use this book

First, look at the contents page opposite. Read the chapter list to see if it includes the subject you want. The list tells you what each page is about. You can then find the page with the information you need.

If you want to know about one particular thing, look it up in the index on page 31. For example, if you want to know about trawlers, the index tells you that there is something about them on page 20. The index also lists the pictures in the book.

When you read this book, you will find some unusual words. The glossary on page 30 explains what they mean.

Series Editor
Margaret Conroy

Book Editor
John Morton

Production
Marguerite Fenn

Picture Research
Kathy Lockley

Factual Adviser
Stephen Riley

Reading Consultant
Amy Gibbs

Series Design
Robert Mathias/Anne Isseyegh

Book Design
Julia Osorno

Teacher Panel
John Allen, Tim Firth,
Bernadette Hill

Illustrations
Tony Gibbons/Linden Artists

Photographs
Associated Press: 25
British Petroleum: 26B, 26-7, 27
British Shipbuilders: 16-17
Bruce Coleman/Jonathon T. Wright: 21
General Dynamics, Electric Boat
Division: 24–25
Robert Harding Picture Library: 10-11,
18-19
National Maritime Museum: 6
Sail Training Association: 28, 28-9
Shell: 15
Sulzer Bros. Switzerland: 17
ZEFA: Cover, 12

CONTENTS

WHY DO WE NEED SHIPS?

The sea and trade

No country can produce all it needs, so countries swap things with each other for money or other goods. This exchange of goods is called trade. Much trade goes by land, but three quarters of the Earth is covered by water and the only way to cross it is by ship or plane. People and small amounts of goods go by plane, but most trade goes by ship.

For hundreds of years goods went in sailing ships. But sailing ships cannot move if the wind blows the wrong way. This makes it hard to travel from certain places, and journeys can be slow and unreliable.

This photo, taken over 60 years ago, shows how dangerous life could be on sailing ships. Large modern ships are usually safe in a storm, particularly if they are far from land and other ships. Why do you think this is so?

Steam engines were invented that could replace sails. But the first steam ships used so much coal that they could not carry enough fuel for long voyages. Even after ships had better engines, sailing ships were cheaper to use if speed was unimportant, and for many more years they carried cargoes like wool, coal, wheat or fertilizer. Eventually, however, sailing ships could no longer compete with steam ships.

There were many different ships. Some carried many people and a little cargo; others carried a lot of cargo and a few people. Some ships ran to timetables, like trains, but others, called tramp steamers, went from port to port, wherever an owner could load or unload a cargo.

Hundreds of kilometres from the nearest land, a tramp steamer with a mixed cargo chugs along while the sailing ship is stuck, 'becalmed' in a windless sea. When they were very young, your grandparents might have seen ships like these.

Getting there safely

Modern ships are strongly built and they rarely sink. Even if a ship does sink, it has lifeboats for all on board and radio messages will soon direct rescuers to find them. But the main reason that shipwrecks are unusual is that the captain always knows exactly where the ship is and can find the safest route.

When you go on a journey by land, you can follow roads and find your way by looking for signposts. You can recognize landmarks like woods or buildings and use them to steer by.

A bird's eye view of what you can see through the window on the ship's bridge on the right.

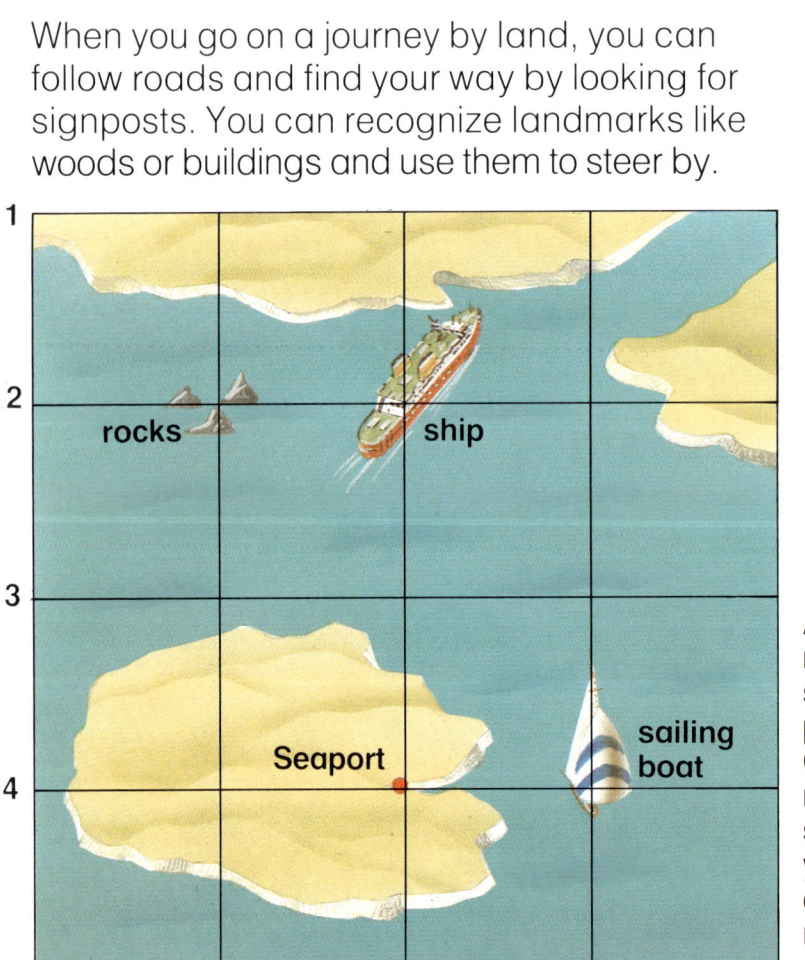

rocks

ship

Seaport

sailing boat

A very simple type of navigation chart, showing a ship's position. The ship is at C2, where the C line meets the 2 line. The sailing boat is at D4. Can you tell where the rocks and Seaport are? Real navigation charts are much more detailed.

radar screen

Sailors run a ship from its bridge, where they can see what is ahead. A radar screen shows a plan of everything around a ship to a distance of about ten kilometres. Radar is very useful at night or in fog.

At sea there is often nothing to see but water and sky. There are sea charts, or maps, but although they tell you important things like how deep the water is, they may show no landmarks for you to recognize. To find your way at sea, you must learn to navigate.

A navigator can find a ship's position at sea by checking where the Sun appears in the sky at noon or where a particular star appears early in the morning. A navigator uses a very accurate clock, called a chronometer, and an instrument called a sextant to make these measurements.

Today you can also find your position by using computers and satellite radio signals. This is most useful in winter, when it is often cloudy. Why do you think satellite navigation is more important in winter than in summer?

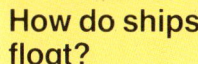

How do ships float?

1 Float an empty metal dish on water. Try to push it into the water. Do you feel something trying to stop you? It's the water pushing up against the empty dish.

2 Now fill the dish with some sand. The sand pushes out the air in the dish, which sinks when the push of the water is not strong enough to hold up the weight of the sand and dish. A ship made of thousands of tonnes of steel floats in the same way, and if you load it too much it sinks.

SHIPS IN TRADE

Passengers afloat

Before there were jets, people crossed the sea in great ships that carried about 1000 crew and 2000 passengers. If you were a passenger it was like being in a luxury hotel with lots of servants. But these ships have all gone because they could not compete with the giant jets which were fifteen times as fast.

Today, the only big passenger ships are cruise liners visiting different ports on holidays at sea. They have shops, a swimming pool and gym, hairdressers, and a cinema and restaurants, so that even at sea there's always something to do. Passengers explore ports when the ship stops, but there's no need for hotels because people sleep on the ship. A favourite winter cruise is to go for a few weeks in the warm Caribbean or Mediterranean Sea. Other cruise liners go north to countries like Norway, where there is beautiful mountain scenery. Do you think liners go to Norway or Iceland in the winter?

Passengers relax on board their ship which is moored off St Lucia, in the Caribbean Sea.

shops

stern

ramp

propellers

main car de

10

Most passenger ships now are ferries which sail back and forth between two or three ports. These ships often carry several hundred people and also have restaurants, duty-free shops, discos and children's playrooms. Most ferries also carry cars, coaches and trucks that can drive on to the ship up a special ramp at the bow and off at the stern through a special door. These are called 'roll-on, roll-off' ferries, or 'ro-ro' ferries for short, and can be loaded and unloaded very quickly.

In the busy summer holidays, this ro-ro ferry could make as many as ten trips a day between England and France.

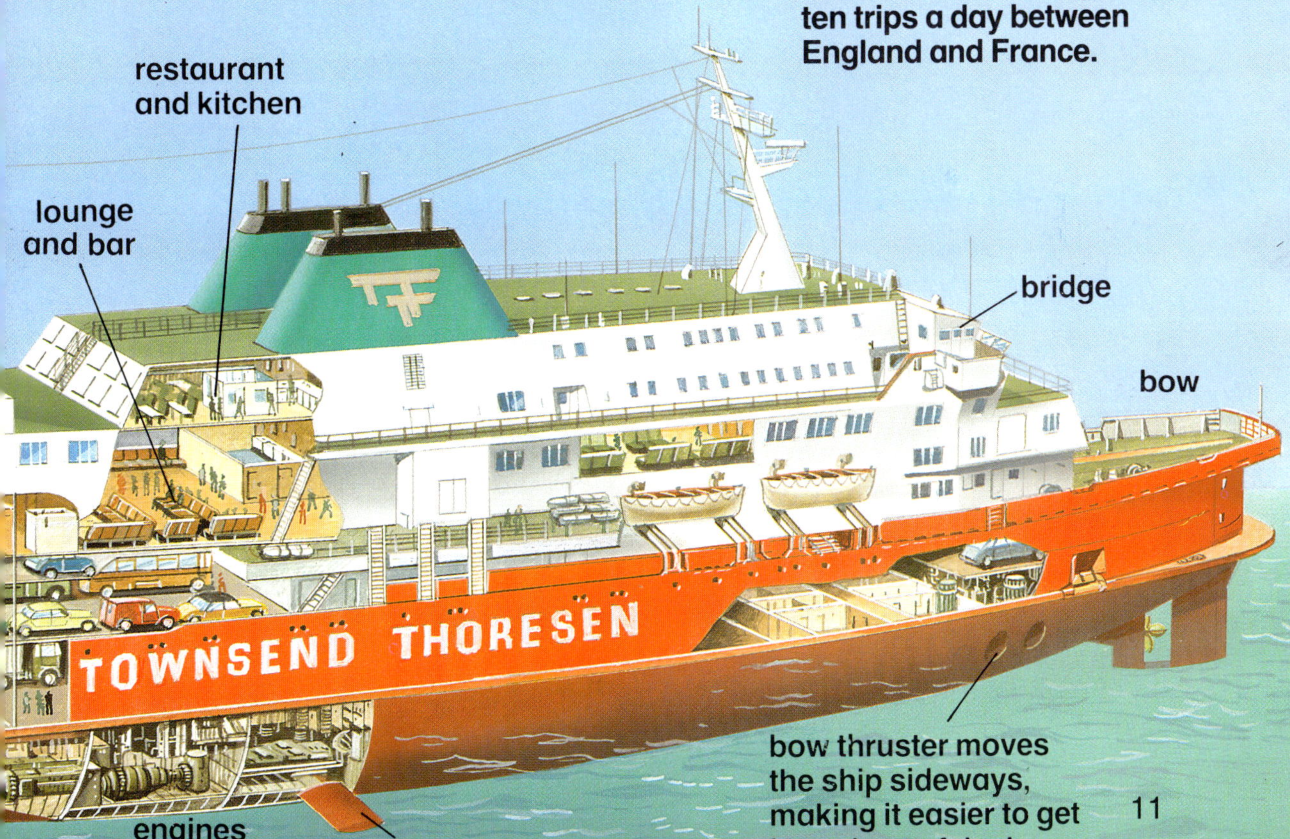

restaurant and kitchen

lounge and bar

bridge

bow

TOWNSEND THORESEN

bow thruster moves the ship sideways, making it easier to get in and out of dock

engines

stabilizer helps to keep the ship steady in rough seas

11

Bananas and trucks

Ships carry an enormous range of cargoes. Rubber, timber and iron ore are just a few of the many raw materials which factories make into things we can use. Materials like cloth or paper have been made in one factory but will go to another to be made into things like clothes or newspapers. Other goods, such as cars or machines, are ready to be sold in shops. See how many foreign cars you can spot on the roads. The cars all came here by ship.

Ships also carry food. Food like meat, wheat or rice must be cooked in a factory or in somebody's home after it has been delivered. Food such as fruit is ready to eat.

growing bananas

banana ship

This ro-ro ship carries over 120 trucks on its top deck. It also has a ramp at its stern for trucks or other vehicles to drive straight onto the lower deck.

12

banana warehouse

buying
a banana

unloading ship
with special
conveyor belt

Most goods sent by sea are loaded into large steel boxes, called containers, to protect them from damage or thieves. Refrigerated containers, 'reefers' for short, keep food fresh.

But some goods do not need to be carried in containers. Instead, they are loaded straight into a ship's hold. These are called bulk cargoes because they are moved in large quantities. Bulk cargoes are either liquids or loose cargoes like coal and grain. They are not easily damaged and can be poured into a ship through a large pipe or on a conveyor belt. Only one of the cargoes in the list at the beginning of this chapter is a bulk cargo that can be poured into a ship. Which is it?

Bananas are picked in the Caribbean Islands when they are hard, green and unripe and are shipped in refrigerated ships. Keeping the fruit cool on the voyage stops it ripening and becoming soft and getting damaged. At the end of a trip the fruit ripens in special warehouses so it finally reaches you in good condition.

Ocean giants

Ships have grown enormously in size over the last 100 years. In their time, people thought that the largest sailing ships were huge, but they were tiny compared with the largest of today's cargo ships and warships.

The world's biggest ships are bulk carriers. Many bulk cargoes are raw materials that few countries can do without. Every country needs oil and although a few countries produce their own, most countries must buy oil from elsewhere.

Oil tankers are the biggest ships of all. Some are longer than three full-size football pitches and the crew get around the decks on bicycles. Ships like this need a circle one kilometre across to turn around in, and if a ship is moving at 20 kph it takes a kilometre to stop.

A truck with a 12-metre-long container.

Giant ships are the cheapest way to carry bulk cargoes. One reason for this is that large ships do not need bigger crews than smaller ships. Only two or three people are needed to keep watch on even the biggest ships. The crew use computers to run and navigate the ship and can control the engines from the ship's bridge. So, although giant ships carry much more cargo, their owners do not have to pay extra wages for a bigger crew.

The *Pamir* was similar to the ship on page six. She was 96 m long.

The *Batillus* is one of the world's largest oil tankers. She is 414 m long.

The *Queen Elizabeth 2* is one of the largest cruise ships. She is 294 m long.

14

The *Enterprise* is an atomic-powered aircraft carrier. She is one of the largest warships ever. She is 342 m long.

Many ports and harbours throughout the world are too small for giant ships to enter when they are fully loaded. Here, the *Batillus*, one of the world's largest ships, is off-loading oil into a smaller, but still large, oil tanker.

ON SHORE

Shipbuilding

Ships used to be built of wood, but about 100 years ago people discovered how to make steel quickly and cheaply. Because steel is stronger than wood, shipbuilders could make much bigger ships. In 1860 a large wooden ship was shorter than a full-size football pitch, but now many modern ships are so long that they would snap in half if they were made of wood.

Modern ships' hulls are built by welding steel plates together. A welder joins the edges of the plates together using a powerful electric current to melt a special rod between them. A welded hull is very strong but it is made even stronger by its steel decks and extra supports inside called bulkheads.

When your grandparents were born there were still a few cargo sailing ships, although by then most ships had large steam engines. Today most ships have diesel engines which give more power for less fuel and take up much less room than steam engines.

The ship's engines are connected to a propeller at the stern, or back, of the ship. The propeller turns round and moves the ship forward by pushing against the water.

Modern ships can be built in parts under cover and welded together later. This picture shows the bridge and living quarters being lowered into place.

bridge

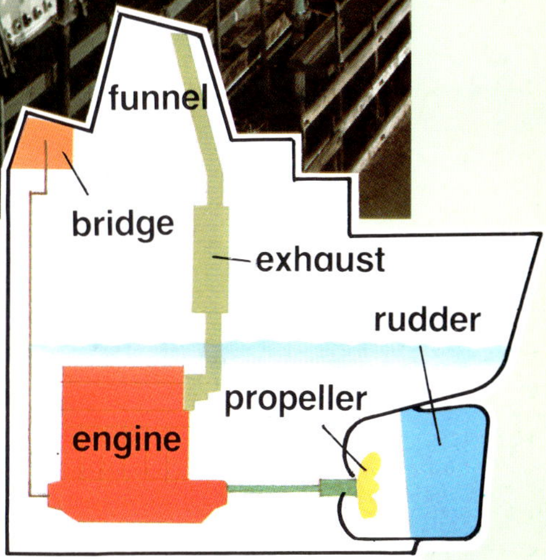

funnel

bridge

exhaust

rudder

propeller

engine

A ship's diesel engine is rather like a diesel engine in a bus, but it is often bigger than a bus! This engine is being checked before leaving the factory.

17

Ports and docks

A port is a place that has everything a ship needs to load or unload its cargo. A hundred years ago there were a few busy ports like New York, London and Calcutta, but most ports were small. Some were just sheltered bits of coast where ships could be unloaded on the beach when the tide was out. When the tide came in again the ship was floated off.

For hundreds of years ports had stone quays, or landing places for ships to tie up to, that were crowded with warehouses. Owners used the warehouses to store their cargoes until they could move them. Hundreds of hard-working dockers loaded and unloaded, bit by bit, cargoes like frozen meat, cotton bales or crates of machinery.

Modern ports are bigger than the old ports and have large deep-water docks where ships can always stay afloat. Thick dock walls protect the ships from storms. On the quays surrounding the docks are cranes and other machinery to unload bulk cargoes or containers.

Container ports have few buildings, as containers do not need to stay under cover. A lot of space is needed to store the containers, and to park trucks, but compared with the old days when dockers loaded cargoes in and out of warehouses, very few people are needed to run a modern port.

In many ports around the world cargoes are still loaded direct from trucks alongside the ships, using dockside cranes and the ships' own machinery. Handling cargo this way often needs large numbers of men and can take a long time. This busy port is Lagos, Nigeria.

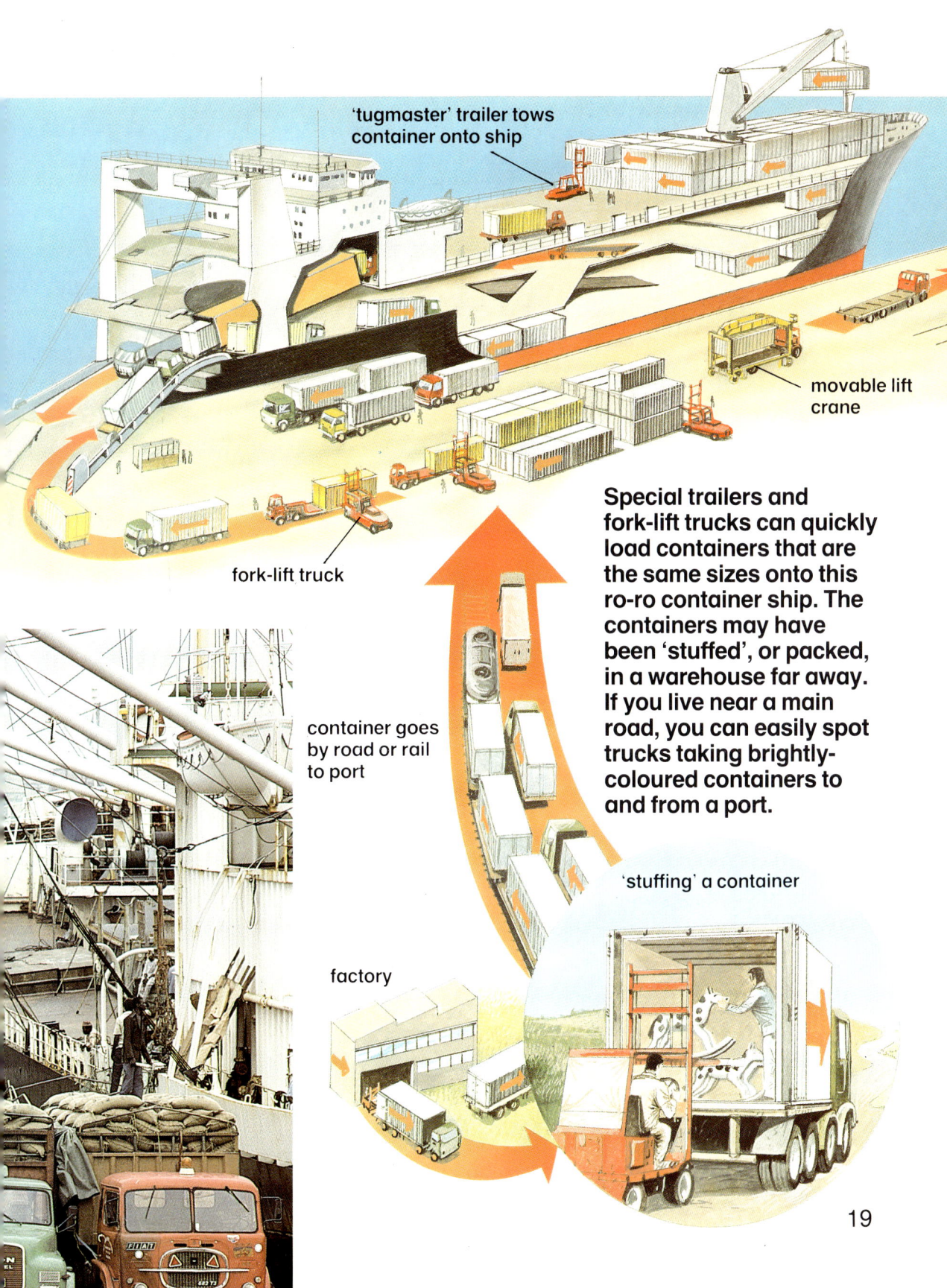

'tugmaster' trailer tows container onto ship

movable lift crane

fork-lift truck

Special trailers and fork-lift trucks can quickly load containers that are the same sizes onto this ro-ro container ship. The containers may have been 'stuffed', or packed, in a warehouse far away. If you live near a main road, you can easily spot trucks taking brightly-coloured containers to and from a port.

container goes by road or rail to port

'stuffing' a container

factory

19

SPECIAL SHIPS

Fishing boats

Some people, such as the Japanese, often eat fish raw; others eat it as fried fish fingers. But however it is eaten, fish is an important food for people all over the world.

Some fish feed near the surface of the sea. Others, such as cod, sole, plaice or haddock, feed lower down or on the sea bed. Different boats and nets are needed to catch different fish. A purse seine net or a ring net catches fish near the surface. One of these giant purse seine nets could hold St Paul's Cathedral. Two ships often work as a pair with these nets, trapping a shoal of fish by drawing the ends of the net around it. The huge catch could weigh as much as 200 cars.

A fishing trawler drags a large net along close to the sea bed. The crew hauls the full net onto the ship so that they can sort and clean the fish before freezing it to keep it fresh until it is sold ashore. Trawlers have a crew of about 25 and are usually larger than seine net boats because they often have to fish further out to sea, sometimes hundreds of kilometres from land. Instead of using nets, some modern boats catch fish by sucking them up from the water. These boats are like huge floating vacuum cleaners.

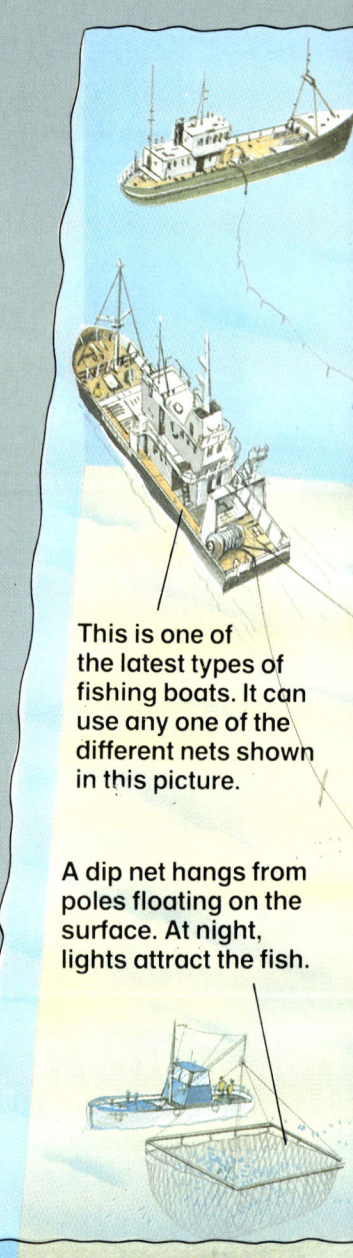

This is one of the latest types of fishing boats. It can use any one of the different nets shown in this picture.

A dip net hangs from poles floating on the surface. At night, lights attract the fish.

Some different fishing boats and nets in use around the world.

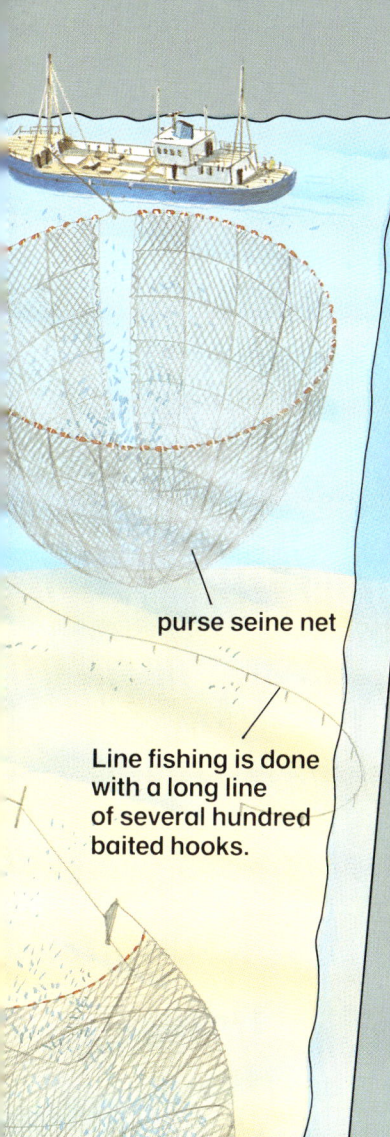

purse seine net

Line fishing is done with a long line of several hundred baited hooks.

trawl net

Modern ships have special electronic equipment which makes it much easier to find shoals of fish. The latest ships can use many different types of net to catch almost any sort of fish. But boats with powerful engines and huge nets have over-fished parts of the sea and some kinds of fish are in danger of becoming extinct.

Hauling in a ring net on a small fishing boat. Far from home, this fisherman's job is hard and dangerous, for he will often have to work in freezing winds and rough, stormy seas.

21

Ships for oil rigs

Your life would be very different without oil. Oil is used mainly to make engine fuel but also for heating and to make plastics, as well as nylon for clothes. How many ways does your family use things that were made from oil? What would it be like without all these things?

The oil your family uses might come from under the sea. Oil wells at sea need many special ships to help them do their work. These ships may be small tankers or tugs to tow out the huge oil rigs which drill or pump. Supply ships carry food and equipment for the rigs. There are also ships that look nothing like ships!

emergency support vessel

trench barge controls 'jet sledge'

Mini-submarine with people on board to check pipe line.

pipe

The 'jet sledge' uses a high-pressure water hose to blast a trench for the pipe.

One of these strange ships is a lay-barge, which lays an oil pipe on the sea bed. It works very carefully so that the pipe does not break in the strong currents. A crane barge has a large crane that can lift the weight of 100 cars. One of its jobs is to lower a diving chamber for divers to work from. Divers may spend several days in a chamber so that they are always ready to be lowered deep down into the sea.

Perhaps the strangest 'ship' is an emergency support vessel, which can deal with almost any accident you could imagine. It can lift heavy machines and send down divers, fight fires, and look after injured people in its own tiny hospital. It has a landing pad for helicopters, which fetch supplies quickly or rescue people in danger.

These are some of the special ships that help get oil from beneath the sea bed and protect the people who do this dangerous work. The lay-barge and the emergency support vessel have underwater pontoons, or floats, which can be filled with water to make the ships steadier in rough seas. This is very useful on the support vessel because emergencies are likely to happen in bad weather. Why do you think the lay-barge has pontoons?

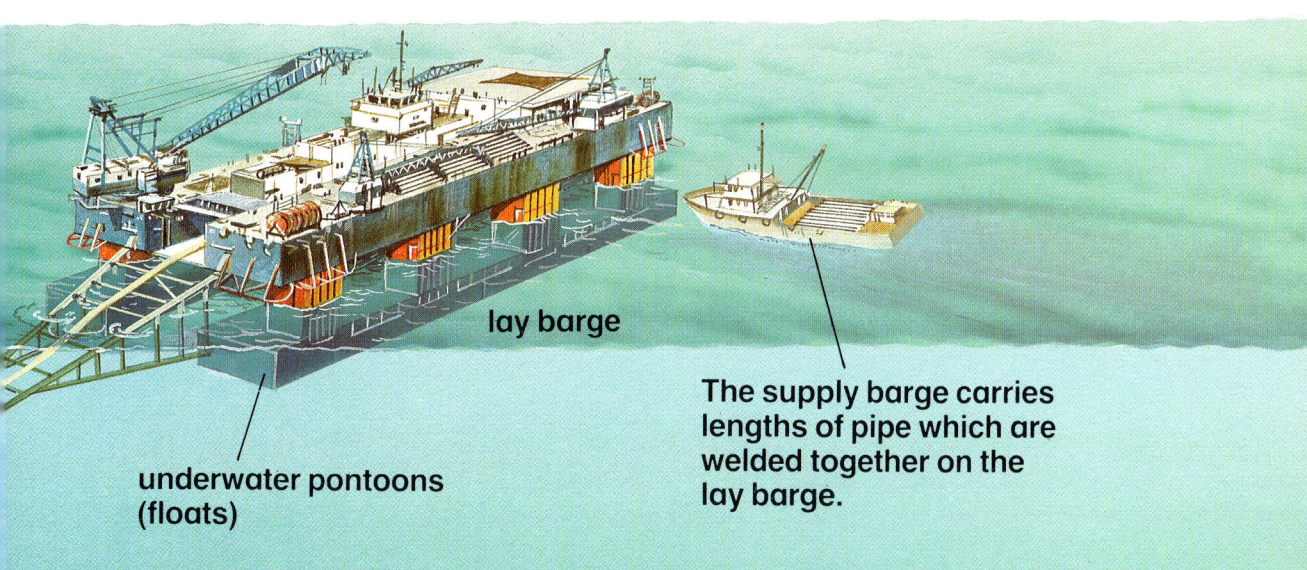

lay barge

underwater pontoons
(floats)

The supply barge carries lengths of pipe which are welded together on the lay barge.

Warships

Warships are ships that carry weapons. They have two main jobs. One is to protect other ships and the other is to protect the people and towns of their country and other friendly countries.

Frigates and destroyers protect cargo ships and aircraft carriers from torpedo or rocket attacks. Aircraft carriers are floating airfields for planes which can fight enemy planes or bomb ships or towns. Warships, especially big ones like aircraft carriers, might be attacked by nuclear weapons, so these ships can be closed off from the outside world and run from inside so that nobody needs to go out into the danger on deck.

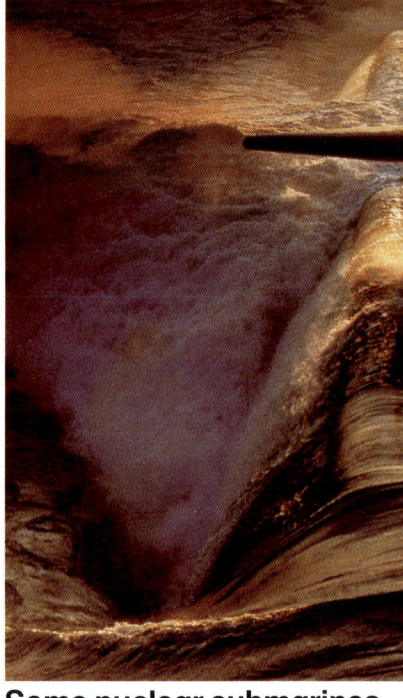

Some nuclear submarines are used to track down and sink enemy ships, especially submarines. They are called 'hunter-killer' submarines.

Destroyers and frigates carry a helicopter to help them find enemy ships and submarines. They also do rescue work. Landing on the moving deck is very difficult and dangerous.

The most important warships are submarines. Most are diesel-powered, but underwater they run on huge batteries because a diesel needs lots of air. The batteries run down after about 18 hours, so the submarine must surface to recharge them with its diesel engines. A few submarines are nuclear-powered and can stay underwater for three months. Some carry missiles which they can launch underwater to destroy a city and its people over 2000 kilometres away.

Although nuclear submarines are huge, they are packed so full of equipment that the crews' living quarters are very cramped. Each member of the crew has a small, cramped bunk and a locker no bigger than a television set in which to keep personal belongings.

In wartime the job of a warship's crew is very dangerous. Missiles or torpedoes can sink their ship and many of the crew could be killed or drowned.

CAPACIDAD

25

PEOPLE AT SEA

Crews

Until just a few years ago, if you worked on a ship your life would have been uncomfortable. Most ships were small but had large crews. Four men might sleep in cramped bunk beds in a tiny room. Modern ships are bigger, but because machines and computers do work that people once did, crews are much smaller.

Machines do so much of the work now that a crew has little to do except when the ship enters or leaves port. The crew will probably have no time to go ashore because ships load and unload as quickly as possible. Ships only make money when they are moving at sea, carrying cargo from one place to another.

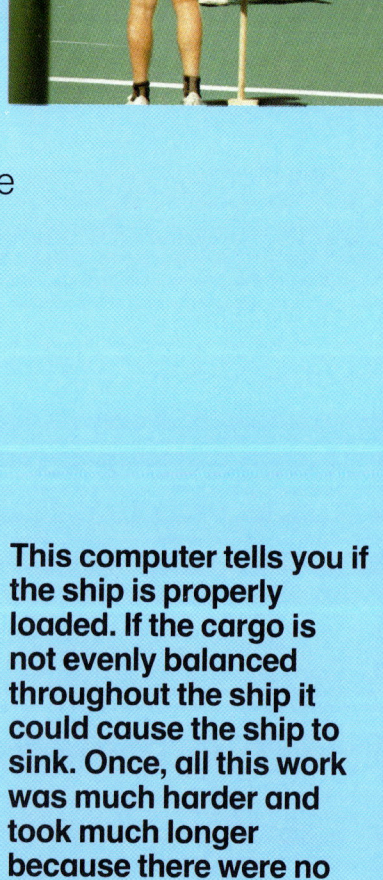

This computer tells you if the ship is properly loaded. If the cargo is not evenly balanced throughout the ship it could cause the ship to sink. Once, all this work was much harder and took much longer because there were no machines to help.

A giant oil tanker is big enough for its crew to relax at a game of deck cricket at sea. Many ships have small swimming pools where the crew can exercise or just enjoy themselves.

Long voyages can be very boring, so ship owners make their ships much more comfortable to live and work in. Members of the crew often have their own air-conditioned cabins and bathrooms, and may even take their husbands or wives along with them on a long trip. The crew can relax and watch video films in the comfort of the ship's lounge.

You might think that you can laze around at sea, but the sea is always dangerous and one mistake can cause an accident. The highly-trained crew have complicated machines to help them do their jobs. But a ship is still run by people and the captain is the most important person on board. A captain must look after the safety of the crew and passengers as well as making sure that the valuable ship and its cargo arrive on time and come to no harm.

Training at sea

Many countries have special colleges or schools where young people can learn to become sailors. These boys and girls, known as cadets, will learn all the usual school subjects, but maths is the most important because later it will help them to learn special skills like navigation. Some countries, like Italy, Sweden, Russia and the USA, keep large sailing ships for cadets to train on for a life at sea.

In a few years' time, you could sail on one of these ships. You'll have a chance to do everything on board and you might even have to work high above the ship, just like the sailors in the photo on page six. You'll be part of a team of young people who must live and work together to do the difficult job of sailing a ship.

Young sailors train on sailing ships but will probably get jobs on diesel-powered ships. But in the future they might work on a ship like this Japanese one. It has engines, but it also has sails which use the wind to help save expensive fuel.

computer-
controlled
sails

JAMDA

NAKAMURA LINE

TANAKA

Cadets work very hard on a training ship. They do unpleasant and boring jobs like cleaning or painting, but they can also do more exciting jobs like navigating or steering the ship.

But even if you don't want to become a sailor you could still go to sea on a training ship. Many countries have sailing ships that boys and girls can take on voyages of two or three weeks. You may not get a job after one of these journeys, but you'll learn a lot about the excitement and dangers of life at sea!

GLOSSARY, BOOKS TO READ

A glossary is a word list. This one explains unusual words that are used in this book.

Bow The front of a ship.
Bridge The ship's bridge is a large room high up in the ship. Through its windows, you get the best view of other ships or rocks in the water around the ship. The crew can control all the important parts of their ship from inside the bridge, including the engine and the steering. Navigation instruments are kept on the bridge.
Bulkheads These are thick steel walls that run from the bottom of the ship to its top deck. They make the ship's hull stronger.
Chronometer A very accurate clock. A navigator needs to know the exact time in order to work out where the ship is.
Navigate To navigate is to find your way from one place to another. Navigation is needed on a journey on land, at sea or in the air.
Radar This uses radio waves to tell the crew about solid things that are near the ship. It can warn of a possible dangerous collision in fog or darkness.
Ro-ro Short for 'roll-on, roll-off', it describes ships which have special ramps for cars, trucks or buses to drive on or off. This is a much quicker way of loading a ship than lifting vehicles on or off by crane.
Satellite navigation A quick, easy and very accurate way to find a ship's position at sea. The ship's radio picks up a special signal from a satellite and a computer works out the ship's position. Ships have to pay for this service.
Sextant This instrument is used to find a ship's position at sea accurately. It measures the angle between the sea horizon, where the sky seems to meet the sea, and where the Sun appears in the sky. The Sun's position changes depending upon the time of the day and the time of the year. You also need a chronometer to work out a ship's position with a sextant.

Stern The back of a ship.
Torpedo A weapon used to sink ships. It is a long tube with a propeller at one end and explosives at the other. Because it travels underwater, it is difficult to see and avoid.
Tramp steamer A cargo ship that sails from port to port, wherever its owner can find a new cargo or needs to deliver one. Tramp steamers do not run to regular timetables.

BOOKS TO READ

Just Look at Water Travel by Bill Gunston, Macdonald Educational, 1986.
Warships by Bill Gunston, Granada, 1983.
Learn about Sailing and Boating by H. Marlow, Ladybird Books, 1979.
See inside an Oil Rig and Tanker by J. Rutland, Hutchinson, 1978.
Seas and Oceans (My First Encyclopedia, volume 7) by Ron Taylor, Macdonald Educational, 1983.
Ships and other Seacraft by Brian Williams, Kingfisher, 1983.